Tiger's Tummy Ache

Written by Lois Bick
Illustrated by Doug Roy

Adams 12 Five Star Schools
1500 E 128th Avenue
Thornton, CO 80241
(720) 972-4000

Tiger was walking along the road.

He saw a little rabbit.

"Oh, boy!" he said.   "Dinner!"

The rabbit hopped away fast.

"Got you!" said the tiger.

"Now I'm going to gobble you up."

Rabbit was little, but he was smart.

"No, no, Mr. Tiger," he said. "Not me.

I am very little. I am very thin.

See? I'm just skin and bones."

"I've got something better to eat," said Rabbit.

"You can join me."

He picked up a few white stones.

"See? Rice cakes."

"How can I eat those?" asked Tiger.

"You just toast them in a fire," said Rabbit.

"When they are red-hot, you gobble them up."

"Here. I'll show you," Rabbit said.

"I know you will enjoy rice cakes."

Now, Tiger wanted to eat the rice cakes
AND the rabbit.

"Okay," he said. "I'll try them."

Rabbit got a fire started.

He put in a lot of stones.

"I've got to get lots of wood for the fire," he said. "You have to keep rice cakes hot, or they will spoil."

Rabbit hopped away, along the road.

Tiger looked at the stones.

They looked nice and hot.

Oh, boy!" he said.

"Rabbit won't miss just one."

And he gobbled one up.

Yipes!

That Tiger got a terrible tummy ache!

And he never tried to eat Rabbit again.